The *reluctant* father

The Reluctant Father
Phillip Toledano

www.thereluctantfather.com
www.mrtoledano.com

First published in the United Kingdom by
Dewi Lewis Media
8 Broomfield Road
Heaton Moor
Stockport SK4 4ND. England
www.dewilewismedia.com
www.dewilewispublishing.com

©2013

for the photographs and main text: Phillip Toledano
for the afterword: Carla Serrano
for this edition: Dewi Lewis Media

ISBN: 978-1-905928-09-5

Design & layout: Phillip Toledano & Dewi Lewis Publishing
Print: EBS, Verona, Italy

The *reluctant* father

Phillip Toledano

dewi lewis media

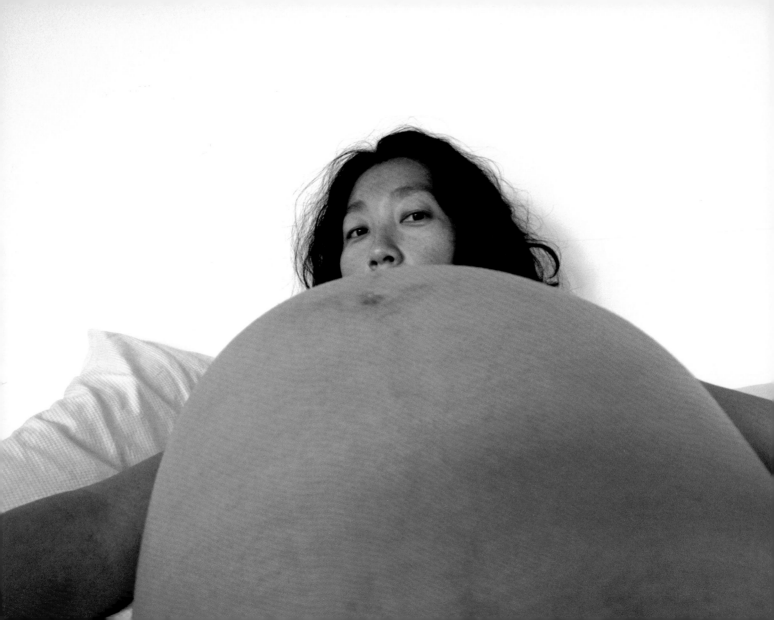

SO THIS IS HOW IT ALL STARTED.

Well, obviously, it's not *exactly* how it started (that would be a slightly different kind of book).

I was never particularly interested in having kids.

I liked them in an abstract sense, in the same way that exercise seems appealing, but in practice, utterly tedious. When friends came over with their kids, I treated them like radioactive material. Tolerable for short periods of time. Prolonged exposure would have unpleasant effects, like hair loss, or inexplicable stains on the sofa.

The problem is, I never took into account the relentless pull of gravity.

You have a girlfriend, and everyone asks, 'So when are you two getting married?'
You get married.
You're married, and everyone asks, 'So when are you two going to have children?'
You have a child.
You have a child, and everyone asks, 'So when are you having the next one?'

Gravity.

When Loulou was born, I was in the delivery room watching the whole thing.

I remember two things.

The sun, rising over the east river, filling the room with a shimmering gold light.

And Loulou. Being pulled out, feet first, like a prize flounder.

I leapt to my feet and uttered a phrase of Churchillian heft: 'Holy shit, she's enormous!'

It's odd. There's how you feel, and then there's how you think you should feel.

In the movies, when people have kids, they're welcomed into the world with a cracking fusillade of manly backslapping and tears. It's one of life's BIG events.

I just felt weird. How could I be a *father*?

Wasn't that something that happened to other people?

To adults?

Was I overwhelmed in a tsunami of love?

Not really.

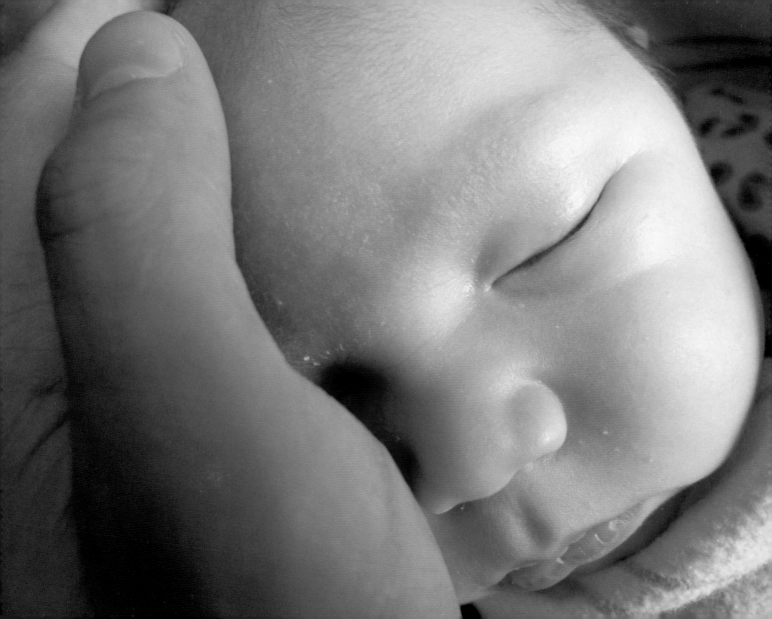

To future fathers: When you're asked how you like being a new dad, follow this script to the letter.

Q: So, how do you like being a father? Do you *love* it?

A: (EYES MISTING OVER SLIGHTLY, AS YOU REACH FOR A HANKIE)
 I'm amazed at the miracle of life. She's so precious! I could look at her *all* day!

I resented the enormous cultural pressure that demanded only one response from me.

When I told people I didn't like it very much, their faces would wrinkle like a walnut. They'd look at me as though I'd taken off all my clothes, and the results were slightly unpleasant.

It wasn't that I didn't feel responsible for Loulou. I was there. To change diapers. To get up in the middle of the night, to do whatever needed to be done. But I felt no emotional connection.

It was like trying to have a relationship with a sea sponge, or a single-cell protozoa.

She didn't DO anything. Or at least, nothing I could understand.

And then there was my wife, Carla.

When Loulou was born, she vanished.

I missed her and me, together.

The infinite space we seemed to have.

The silence.

The casual elasticity of our lives.

I could turn around, and see it, dwindling, small, behind us.

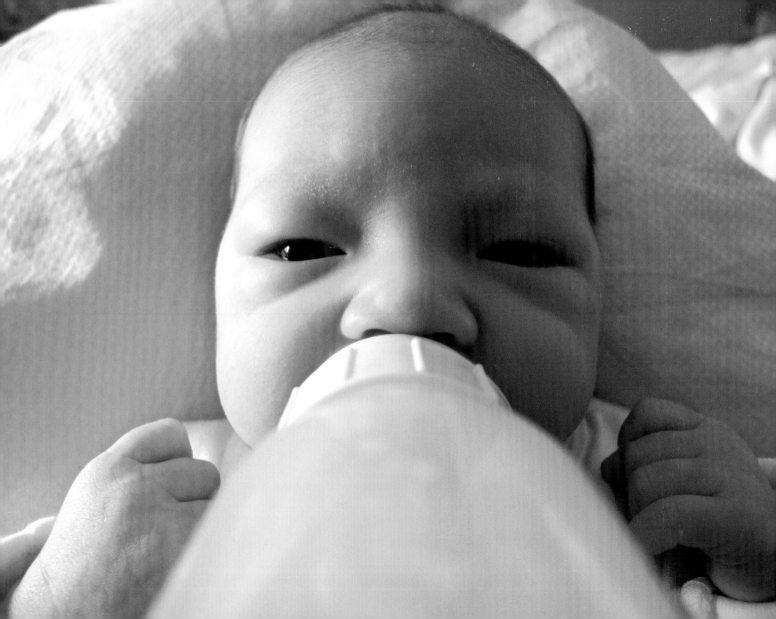

I had been downsized.

Meet my replacement: The alien.

Take me to your leader.

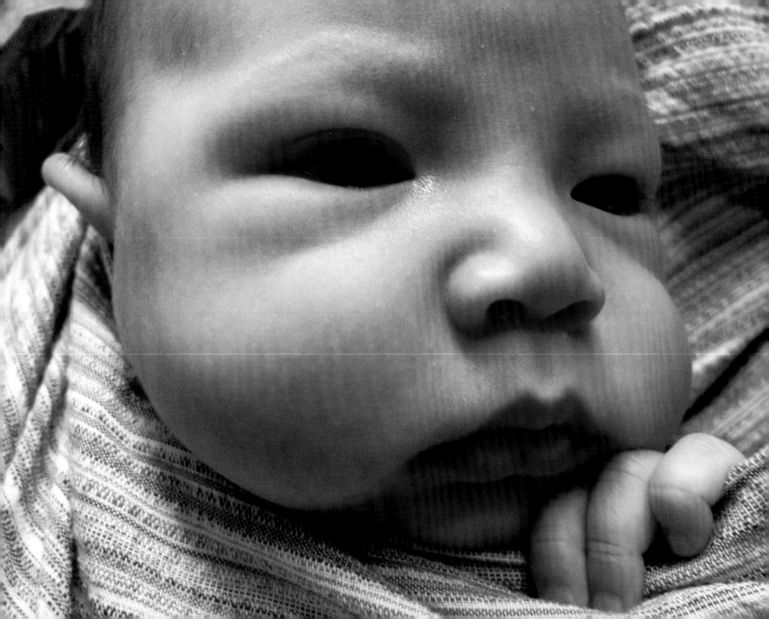

Also, sleep is cancelled for the next three years.

Everything Loulou did was utterly incomprehensible.

Take eating, for instance.

It was like watching a wildlife documentary. She'd savage the nipple (rubber, or Carla) with a crazed animal ferocity, and then slip into a deep opiate slumber, mouth agape.

I imagined myself doing the same at a dinner party.

Slumped over half-eaten meatloaf, a thick rope of drool gently swaying from my bottom lip.

The first time I heard Loulou sneeze,

I was so happy.

Something human, that I could relate to!

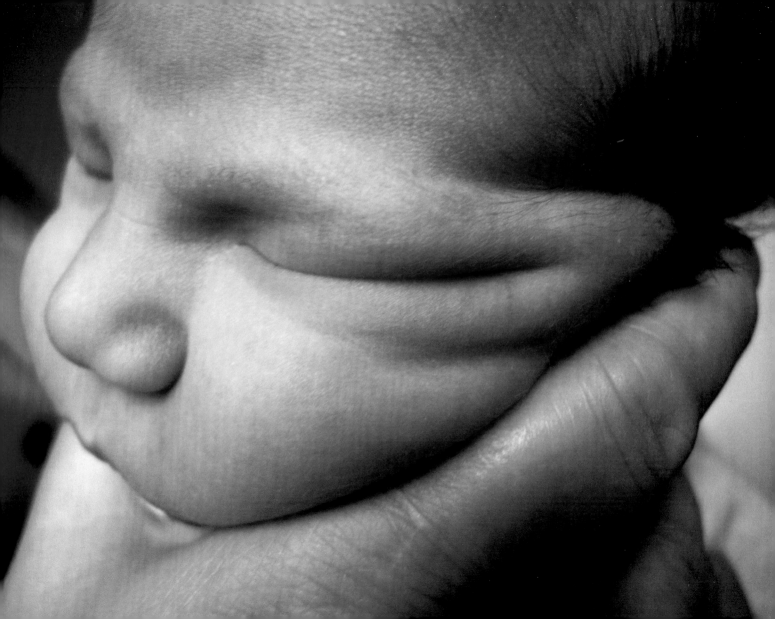

Even our dog had no interest in Loulou.

Except for when she was eating.

Then Georgie was utterly mesmerized.

She would vacuum up every morsel of culinary shrapnel in the fifteen foot blast radius.

Handling a baby was like working with highly unstable explosives.

I would lower Loulou gingerly into the crib.

The slightest movement and....BOOOOM!

I'd be frantically looking for a way to diffuse the infant.

GREEN WIRE OR RED WIRE?! WHICH ONE DO I CUT?

I would fly into a multi-armed panic.

Does she need milk? Has she crapped her pants? Is she too hot? Too cold?

WHAT'S WRONG?! SHE WAS JUST SOUND ASLEEP!

I remember mentioning to Carla that the screaming was making me crazy.

She said 'I know, doesn't it just break your heart?'

I meant *throwing the baby out the window* crazy.

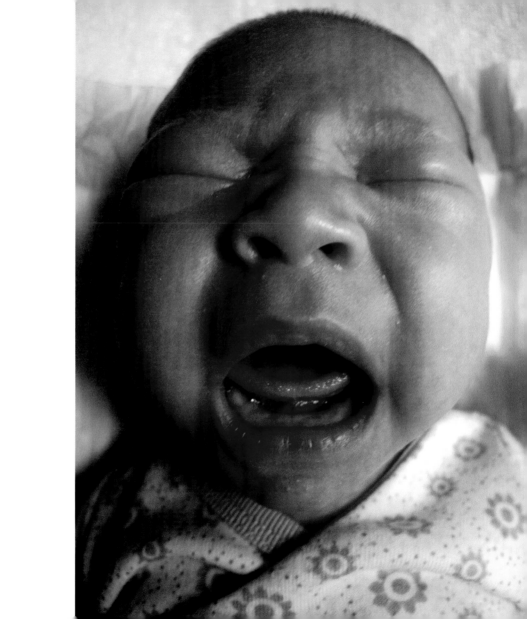

Some men deal with their baby rage by drinking.

I made plates.

I thought this was high comedy, but Carla was not amused.

For a long time, when people asked to see a photo of Loulou, this was what I'd show.

The contrarian in me liked not displaying the usual cherubic imagery.

Oh how adorable! It's a photo of Loulou poking her head out of a casserole pot!

Do all baby pictures have to be carved out of a block of solid saccharin?

Weather forecast:

Chance of heavy precipitation: 100%

Almost worse than the screaming was the anticipation.

Especially when you're lying in bed, at 2am.

Was that snort the beginning?

Would it last ten minutes, or two hours?

Apparently one of the reasons women can handle the endless din
is because nature anesthetizes them with soothing hormones, making
the cacophony not only bearable, but a musical delight!

Surely a pharmaceutical conglomerate could make a patch for men to
wear on their arm, so we're less homicidal when the siren goes off?

Let's not forget the baby industrial complex.

A baby wipe warmer?

Would Loulou sue her parents later on because she'd been emotionally devasted by the use of room-temperature tissues on her (admittedly cute) gluteus maximus?

Don't forget the baby-bottle sterilizer?

The ONLY defense against a Mongol horde of enraged germs, honor bound to infect the baby with explosive diarrhea.

Even worse were the product-zombie parents, who swore that their child would not be alive today were it not for the 'Yoga for toddlers' DVD boxed set.

I understood that babies like bright colors. Or at least, toy companies think they do. But are there any toys available that don't make you feel seasick, or make you convulse like a landed haddock?

Does your child's future hinge on what choice you make, every time you buy her a toy?

Would buying the *'Incomparable baby-genius mobile'* versus the *'Astonishing-prodigy infant squeeze-ball'* really make the difference between Harvard, or rooting about in the trash for a half-eaten tuna sandwich?

Why do babies really need *so* much stuff? What's wrong with a stick? Or a nice bucket of dirt?

(When you've only been alive for 5 months, isn't *everything* entertaining?)

Having said that, let me just contradict myself by saying that I would have done ANYTHING, bought ANYTHING, if I'd thought it would have made Loulou sleep more and scream less.

I used to look down on parents who would put their kids in front of the tv, just for a moment's peace.

I have a quite different opinion, now.

I'm English. I'm not frightened by death, or the shame of a large urine spot on my trousers.

It's *making a scene in public.*

So you can imagine how I felt traveling with Loulou.

What if she went full Plácido Domingo on the plane?

Suddenly, I was the buffoon with an air-raid siren for a child.

Everyone staring. And me, grinning idiotically like a circus chimp, mumbling *'sorry, sorry, sorry'*.

Loulou's arrival really made me consider my own mortality.

When she turns 20, I'll be 60.

Will I seem like an old man to her?

Confused by what she wears, how she talks?

Will she roll her eyes, and say 'oh dad...'

Or will we be friends? Drinking cups of tea in the kitchen, talking about the latest boyfriend?

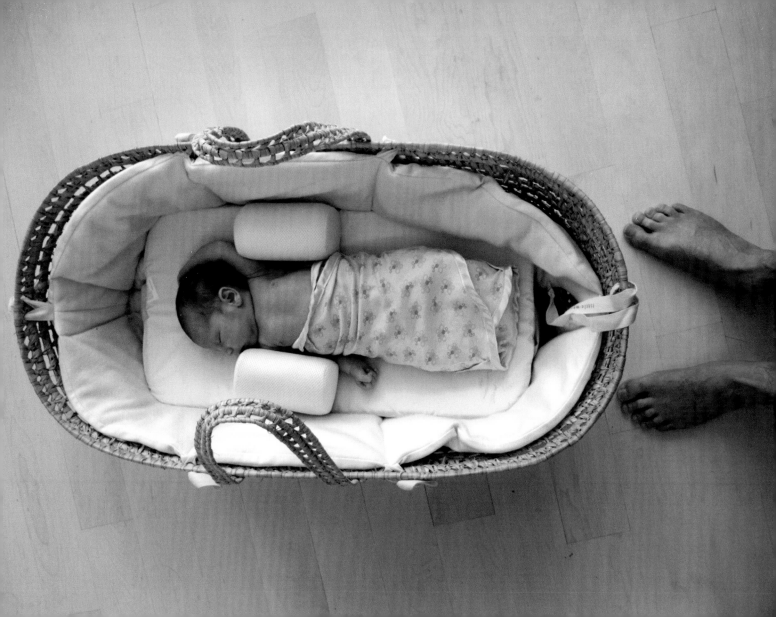

Both of my parents died in the last four years. In fact, my father died four months before Loulou was born.

Oddly enough, her arrival has made their absence even more tangible.

There are so many things I wish I could ask my mother.

How was I at her age? Did I do this? Did I do that?

I just wish she was here to explain the inexplicable.

To tell me that everything will be ok, that I'll understand, in time.

And of course, I think about my father. He loved children so much, and Loulou would have filled him to the brim.

When you have a child, she becomes your past, present and future. I not only see myself and Carla in Loulou, but I see my parents too.

It gives me such joy, to see them alive, in her.

It's sad, but I realize as I get older that all clichés are true.

I do something I said I'd NEVER do:

Baby photos.

It's really quite embarrassing.

When I meet other parents, I lunge for the iphone. I can't WAIT to bore people.

'Look, I know you don't like baby pictures, but Loulou is different!'

I'm that sad statistic. The proud father.

I look back at all these photographs, and see how they reveal my slow and inevitable metamorphosis.

From bewildered observer, to eager participant.

From photographer, to father.

At the beginning of this book, I spoke about gravity.

Love also has its own gravitational pull, and naturally, it was inevitable that I would succumb.

When people told me that my life would change when Loulou started to smile, they were right.

Humor is how I connect with the world.

It's my language.

So when Loulou began to speak that language to me, it was pretty extraordinary.

The first time I teased her, and she teased me back, I cried.

We understood each other.

It amazes me.

There is such a sense of love in these pictures that wasn't there before.

I want to end with an apology to Carla.

I know that my candor was often hard to hear. I was so committed to the idea of honesty, that I forgot about *her* truth. The marvel of Loulou. The unalloyed joy of being a mother.

Also, I want to apologize to Loulou.

One day, she'll see these photographs, and read these words.

I want her to know that even though I found the beginning of her life quite bewildering, I'm so glad she's here now.

I love you very much Loulou.

While I'm at it, I'd like to say something to the future Loulou.

Please don't wear sweatpants with the letters 'JUICY' stitched on the bum.

Please don't become a goth, or an emo (or whatever they'll be doing in 15 years), and peer at me gloomily through six layers of black eyeshadow.

Remember. Before your father was a parent, he was a person.

Young, and confused, just like you.

To my parents.

I wish you'd gotten a chance to meet your granddaughter.

I miss you both, and I tell Loulou about you often.

I think about all you gave me, and hope that I can give the same to her.

A FEW WORDS FROM THE MRS...

When Phil and I were first married, we always promised ourselves that we would stay objective and real when we had kids. We made a pact that we would tell each other if the baby was weird-looking. We agreed never to force our friends to look through very ordinary pictures of our 'extraordinary' child. We pledged never to create an excruciatingly long voicemail greeting recorded by an incomprehensible toddler. But then, something happened. I gave birth.

The first time I held her, I was propelled forward by the force of maternal love and instinct. Loulou wasn't exactly beautiful as a newborn. I can say that now, but back then, she was light shimmering in the sea on a perfect day. I moved ahead in blind awe of Loulou but Phil, well, it was as if he stayed put.

Instead of reveling in fatherhood, Phil defied it with a creative vengeance. When people asked to see a picture of Loulou, he would show them a red-faced moon screaming in fury which he'd conveniently printed on a tote bag. When friends asked what it was like to be a father, he would answer with brutal honesty about how totally unfulfilling it is for the dad because the 'sea sponge' just wanted mom. When we fought under the strain of fresh parenthood, he would desperately try to coax me into admitting that some part of this experience was shit, kind of shit...maybe a little shit?

At the time, all I wanted was for Phil to play along like the other new fathers. All of them memorized the script: 'It's the best thing I ever did', 'Fatherhood is amazing', 'Great!–I'll take the 4am shift!' But not my contrarian, forthright Phil. I fell in love with him because he fought conformity, but now I was desperate for him to join the ranks of smiling Stepford dads.

It's ironic that I am writing the afterword to this book because our first year as parents was especially difficult and I would never have imagined showcasing that to the world. Both stubborn, we took our sides of light and dark to surreal extremes; mine spent in a world of sugar coated baby-talk, his in a dungeon of screaming and excrement.

I don't really know when we found the bridge but we did. And now I can laugh at the past in technicolor amnesia.

I think this book is proof of that.

Carla Serrano

To Carla. My sweet Carla. Who puts up with far more than she should. I love you.

To Loulou, of course, who unwittingly provided such magnificent material for this book.
My heart bursts when I look at you.

To Tim and Tita. For stepping in when my parents couldn't. For loving a slightly odd son-in-law.
And for always fixing things.

To Tsering. Loulou loves you very much. We could never have done it without you.
You're part of the family, always.

To Annie. Thank you for allowing me to say the things I couldn't say to your sister.

And to my parents. I wish you could be here. It would have made me very happy to see
you both holding my daughter in your arms.